Inside The

™

The Complete User's Guide

Inside The

MAGIC 8 BALL™

The Complete User's Guide

THE TOY WITH ALL THE ANSWERS

by Miriam Zellnik

Magic 8 Ball © 2002 Mattel, Inc.

RUNNING PRESS

PHILADELPHIA · LONDON

Library of Congress Cataloging-in-Publication Number 2001094131

ISBN 0-7624-1224-0

Cover and interior design by Alicia Freile
Edited by Nancy Armstrong and Molly Jay
Typography: AdLib, Concorde, Helvetica Condensed, and Brush Script

This book may be ordered by mail from the publisher.
Please include $2.50 for postage and handling.
But try your bookstore first!

Running Press Book Publishers
125 South Twenty-second Street
Philadelphia, Pennsylvania 19103-4399

Visit us on the web!
www.runningpress.com

"For All Those Who Believe that Their Lives are Directed By the Vagaries of Fortune"

—Quote from the original Syco-Seer packaging design

Special Thanks

To Nancy Armstrong, a fine editor and friend. To all those associated with Alabe Crafts, especially Anne Korey, Don and Lowell Bookman, Ken Korey, and Gail and David Berwald. To the folks at the Cincinnati Public Library in general, and to Andy Balterman specifically. To the women of the Well. To all my friends in Portland, who listened to me natter on about Magic 8 Ball toys long past the point when most people's eyes would glaze over. To Adrian, for everything

Contents

A True Fascination... 8

The History of the Magic 8 Ball........................ 12

The Later Years... 42

Magic 8 Ball Fun Facts!................................. 50

The Magic 8 Ball Aptitude Test........................ 54

Talking to Past Celebrities.............................. 58

Magic 8 Ball Terminology............................... 62

As long as mankind has had the gift of language, people have tried to predict the future, using everything from tea leaves to fortune-telling. Come to think of it, for all we know, even pre-verbal cave people might have looked into piles of sticks and pebbles for clues to their lives ("Should I eat the deer or the elk meat?" or "Does Ug like me or is he just using me?" etc.). From crystal balls to sundials, people clamor for objects that will give them guidance.

Sid Korey (left) and Abe Bookman.

Perhaps all other forms of prognostication were leading toward the moment when a man in Cincinnati looked deep into himself and had a vision, a vision about a new way that people would be able to see the future. And what he saw was . . . a billiard ball. And not just any billiard ball, but an 8 ball, one that had many answers contained within. This ball would be a novelty paperweight that would always be ready to dispense wisdom. All it asked of you was a gentle shake, and your most pressing question—to which it would reply with a yes or no answer.

5 Questions Never To Ask Your 8 Ball

1. Is he (she) cheating on me?
2. Are people talking about me behind my back?
3. Should I buy that stock?
4. Should I sell that stock?
5. Am I ugly?

WONDERFUL FUN - CLEVER DECORATION

FORTUNE TELLING GAME

THE *Magic Eight Ball!*

$1.98

You'll enjoy asking the Magic Eight Ball questions about the future. You'll be amazed at the mysterious way it answers them. Use it over and over again with as much entertainment and surprise. Besides, you'll find it an unusual decorative piece or paper weight for the home or office.

Fun
•
Mystery
•
Beauty

THE HISTORY OF THE
Magic 8 Ball

Alabe Crafts and the Syco-Seer

The year was 1946. World War II had recently ended, and in Cincinnati, Ohio, a man named Max Levinson owned a store called Marshall's, where he sold furniture and clothing. Max was a natural salesman, outgoing and always interested in people. A customer would come into the store, or a vendor would drop off an order, and Max would come out from behind the counter and they would get to talking. One day, Al Carter, a part-time electrician and handyman Max did business with,

showed him a small toy he had invented. Turns out Al was more than a handyman, he was also a "mad genius inventor" sort of guy. He had brought one of his creations in that day, and Max was intrigued. He had never seen anything like this toy.

Albert C. Carter was an interesting fellow. With a professional fortune-teller for a mother, perhaps it's no wonder that he had come up with this little gizmo he called the "Syco-Seer." It was a cylindrical object, sort of like a jar, with a laminated paper cube inside that had answers about the future printed on each side. The original impetus for his idea came from his mother, Laura (Mary) Carter Pruden, who was a Cincinnati medium of considerable renown.

Rumor had it that Arthur Conan Doyle, author of the Sherlock Holmes stories, frequently sought advice from Laura. Her specialty was "slate writing," in which a blackboard was placed in a box. A clairvoyant would then drop a piece of chalk into the box and seal it, at which point the spirits would miraculously write an answer on the slate. Al Carter watched his mother amaze her clients with her uncanny talents, and he came up with the idea of using a magic slate as a toy.

Instead of a box and chalkboard, he put his pre-written slate into a jar, suspended in a thick liquid he called "Ectomite" to add to the mystery. If you asked it a question, the Syco-Seer would tell you an answer as the slate rose to the surface of the liquid to

Magic Window

The original window in the Magic 8 Ball was called the "spirit slate" and it used to protrude slightly. Later design changes made it to an "innie" that is recessed from the surface of the ball. Also, the original glass was replaced with a strong plastic in later versions of the ball.

Max Levinson

Sid Korey

display its writing. It was this prototype of the Syco-Seer that Al brought into work one day at Marshall's Department Store. Max Levinson looked at the toy, and thought about how many of his customers might enjoy this novelty item.

He talked to his family about it, especially his brother-in-law, Abe Bookman, a manager at the store, to whom Al had also shown his prototype. Now, Abe was a bit of a mechanical genius in his own right. He had graduated from the Ohio Mechanics Institute, and always had a way with all kinds of machines, not just cars. When he saw the Syco-Seer, he too saw the possibilities of the toy. More than that, he saw improvements and innovations that could make it even better.

After some discussion, Max Levinson decided to start a company called Alabe Crafts (named for *Al* Carter and *Abe* Bookman). Al would be a silent partner and Abe would actually run the company. Sid Korey, Max's son-in-law, joined the firm as the sales and marketing manager. Al Carter's original was a "crude model of tin and glass," according to a history Sid Korey wrote many years later, and the first order of business was to ready it for the marketplace.

Abe and Al spent many weekends tinkering with the prototype fortune-teller. According to the history of the Magic 8 Ball written in the 1960s by Sid Korey, "The gadget absorbed an unbelievable amount of money and work and thought before it became patentable and was ready to market."

Abe Bookman

Alabe Crafts

Be Sincere!

Instructions reproduced verbatim from the original Alabe Crafts Syco-Seer toy:

"Be sincere! Ask only questions regarding the future—the past you already know. Do not ask the same question twice (unless told to do so by the "SYCO-SEER") as the first one you receive is the one intended for that particular question. Trick questions and the like will prove your insincerity and the answers you receive will not be reliable." "Within a short time the "SYCO-SEER" answer to your question will appear on the tiny slate controlled in Ectomite. The same procedure applies in asking each question. Your answers will not always appear in the same given time. If you receive no answer within 30 seconds, the power is temporarily obstructed, so ask your question again."

"The SYCO-SEER answers all questions: WHAT? WHEN? WHERE? WHICH? WHO? HOW? For those who believe that their lives are directed by the vagaries of fortune . . . For those who feel that they possess a controlling influence or receive guidance from the subconscious or supernatural . . ."

However, after much work, Abe Bookman finally figured out a manufacturing process, and the toy became the first item in the Alabe Crafts catalogue. Alabe called it the Syco-Seer, but it soon morphed into a slightly different toy called the Syco-Slate, also known as the "Pocket Fortune Teller".

Al Carter's Decline

Unfortunately, Al Carter never did get his personal or professional life in order and work productively for the company that bore his name. He died in the late 1940s, and did not live to see his idea redesigned as the best-selling Magic 8 Ball toy. At the time of his death, his landlady threw out all of his work, including some of his prototypes and plans for other inventions, such as an

When my friends and I drove from Ohio to San Francisco after we graduated college, we often used the Magic 8 Ball to decide what routes to take, what exits to get off at to stretch, what restaurants to stop off at and so on and so forth. It livened up the trip!

R____, San Francisco

electric combination lock (something that had never before
been attempted). However, his contribution to the now famous
Magic 8 Ball lives on.

The Syco-Slate

Back at Alabe Crafts, one of the first things Abe did was change
the design of the Syco-Seer so that instead of two ends of a
cylinder, each with a window to view the answer cube, only one
side would be a window. Alabe marketed this new version as
the Syco-Slate. The original black and gold package had an
astrology chart on one side and lettering proudly proclaiming
"Syco-Slate: The Pocket Fortune-Teller" on the other.

In Al Carter's original prototype, the jar had been filled with
molasses, which sounds funny but was actually an ingenious
design. Unlike water, molasses wouldn't freeze easily, so when
the toy was exposed to heat or cold, the jar wouldn't crack open.

But there was always room for improvement, and since Abe
was a scientist, there was nothing he liked better than going off

BE YOUR OWN
FORTUNE TELLER!
with the New
Syco Slate
POCKET FORTUNE TELLER

"ANSWERS"
TO YOUR QUESTIONS ABOUT THE FUTURE!

SEE IT DEMONSTRATED!

Syco Slate
THE POCKET
FORTUNE
TELLER

What's In It?
A Brief History of Goo

♦ Al Carter's original toy was filled with molasses. Unlike water, molasses wouldn't freeze easily, so when the toy was exposed to heat or cold, the jar wouldn't crack open.

♦ When Abe Bookman redesigned it as "the Syco Seer," he changed the formula to be a sort of generic anti-freeze: a mixture of isopropyl alcohol, invert sugar, antifreeze, and blue dye.

♦ At some time during the period when Tyco Toys, Inc. made the Magic 8 Ball, the formula was changed again to meet more stringent safety standards in the toy industry.

♦ Mattel's current formula is a closely guarded secret.

into the lab and tinkering with a product. Over the next several months, he developed a new liquid to fill the toy, one that acted as an antifreeze so that even in a frigid dock warehouse in the middle of winter, no freezing would occur. He finally settled on a mixture of isopropyl alcohol, invert sugar, antifreeze, and dye.

He then replaced the original laminated paper cube with the 20-sided icosahedron, writing the various answers with help from Sid Korey.

Abe and Sid consulted with Dr. Lucien Cohen, a psychology professor at the University of Cincinnati, to research what ratio of positive, negative, and ambiguous responses

23

were the most favorable. Based on what he told them, they developed the answers used to this day, some of which are below:

♦ Signs point to Yes

♦ Reply hazy try again

♦ Without a doubt

♦ My sources say No

♦ You may rely on it

♦ Outlook not so good

♦ Better not tell you now

Many Hours In The Laboratory

When it came time to put the answers on the "cube," Abe ran into a problem. Originally, the white script-style letters had been etched or stamped on to the grey paper cube, but the new poly-

Magic 8 Ball Timeline

Of all the mysteries surrounding the Magic 8 Ball, perhaps there is none more frustrating than the fact that no one seems to know the exact year of its invention. Like the source of its power, the exact origin of the ball is shrouded in mystery. Here is a possible timeline; no records exist of exact dates, so a range is given based on several sources:

1946 Max Levinson puts up the money to start a new business—Alabe Crafts.

1946 or 1947? Alabe produces its first product, the Syco-Seer.

1947 or 1948? Alabe changes the Syco Seer to be half the size, and markets it as the Syco Slate, a pocket fortune-teller.

1948 or 1949? Abe Bookman and Sid Korey redesign the Magic 8 Ball shape.

1971 Alabe Crafts is sold to the Ideal Toy Company.

1987 Tyco Toys, Inc. acquires Ideal Toys.

1997 Mattel, Inc. acquires Tyco Toys.

THE NEW **SYCO SLATE** POCKET FORTUNE TELLER

...own Fortune Teller

ethylene surface of the answer cube was too smooth–there was no way to print on it, since normal inks would not adhere to its plastic surface. So off to the lab he went, whole days spent mixing inks and lampblack and all variety of dyes. Sounds like messy work, but in fact, "messy" was the antithesis of Abe's style.

Although the laboratory and toy shop were filled with grease-stained machinery, not to mention all those black pigments, the thing about Abe Bookman was his careful cleanliness at work. Fifty years later, his son Don Bookman still remembers his father coming home from work with "not a spot on his clothing, and he always wore a white shirt. Not even a spot on his hands."

There at the lab, with his beakers and test tubes, he came up with the answer–a new kind of ink that would print on polyethylene! This was a great breakthrough, and in fact, Abe Bookman is in the DuPont Hall of Fame for this invention, which had uses far beyond the humble Magic 8 Ball. To this day, many of the plastic squeeze bottles you see on grocery store shelves use the patented ink that Abe Bookman invented for his "answer cube" printing.

Abe Bookman and the Alabe team of scientists were constantly working to improve their question-answering toy. A better lid and gasketing arrangement made the liquid less prone to air bubbles, an ongoing concern of Abe, who felt that bubbles made the toy look "tacky." But the main thing that Abe felt needed an overhaul was the jar-like casing itself. The "Pocket Fortune Teller" was interesting, but he felt there must be a better shape for the toy. . . The question was: What?

The Rush For Fortune-Telling Toys

Post-World War II was a time of great hope and renewal in America, and the toy market really took off as people turned away from the rationing and seriousness of wartime, and toward a future filled with new homes, new jobs, and new children. The Syco-Seer and Syco-Slate toys were hard to describe, but once they were seen in action, they engaged people. It is human nature to want to see into the future, so one of the marketing techniques was to have actresses dressed as Gypsies and fortune-

Magic 8 Ball Techniques

While the instructions tell you to turn ball over gently, some people insist that it's the special shake that gives the Magic 8 Ball its eerie accuracy. Below, some techniques for getting the most out of your Magic 8 Ball:

♦ The Closed-Eye Shuffle: Ask question. Shut eyes as you gently cradle the Magic 8 Ball in both hands and move it side to side. Turn over to reveal answer as you open your eyes.

♦ The Cocktail Shaker: Shake ball up and down vigorously for 30 seconds. Ask question aloud as you turn the ball over to reveal answer.

♦ The Simple Turnover: Ask question with ball on table face down in front of you. Pick it up and turn it over to reveal answer.

♦ The Partner Prognostication: Ask question out loud to a second person. (Alternatively, think of question silently.) The second person turns over the Magic 8 Ball and reads the answer out loud to you.

tellers in department stores, touting the Alabe product line.

By 1947, this technique was working almost too well. Stores in Chicago and New York had hordes of shoppers coming to see the "gypsy girls" scantily clad in their gauzy outfits, displaying the many charms of the Pocket Fortune-Teller. At Goldblatt's of Chicago, the fire marshal was called at one point to shut down the store, as the capacity of the building was exceeded.

Unfortunately, without expensive promotional campaigns, the Syco-Slate was just a novelty item that didn't have the "pizzazz" needed to catapult it into truly stratospheric toy sales. The real surge of popularity didn't happen until a year or two later.

I've had a Magic 8 Ball in my law office for almost four years, and practically every lawyer I've ever worked with, no matter how strait-laced, has at some point come in, picked it up, and asked it for advice as to how to proceed with a case. (I don't think that made it into the billing descrip-tion to the client!)

J____, Lawyer

The Magic 8 Ball Arrives

It was either in 1949 or 1950 when the now-famous Magic 8 Ball case was added to Alabe's pocket fortune-telling toy. Sid Korey is generally credited with the flash of inspiration that led to the Magic 8-ball shape being adopted. Whether Sid came up with this idea one day out of the blue, or whether he and Abe and other Alabe employees had meetings and discussions, we will never know for sure.

One possible scenario is this: Brunswick Billiards had commissioned Alabe to make a novelty for them, so the idea of using various balls as fortune-tellers was floating around the Alabe offices. At the time, the saying that someone in a troublesome position was "behind the 8 ball" was popular, and something about the perfectly smooth shiny black pool ball with its distinctive number 8 added the perfect touch to the fortune-telling toy.

In a 1973 interview, Sid Korey reminisced about the derivation of the now-classic Magic 8 Ball design: "We just figured, after all, everybody's either behind the 8 Ball or in the

Sid Korey (left) and Abe Bookman.

doghouse somehow." And so the toy was born. With its flattened side and pleasing heft, the ball made a perfect paperweight. Soon, the Alabe factory in Cincinnati was turning out as many Magic 8 Balls as they could.

Unlike the short life-span of most fad toys, the Magic 8 Ball retained its popularity season after season. After a brief overlap, the Syco-Slate Pocket Fortune-Teller was phased out and the Magic 8 Ball became the company's biggest and most long-standing seller.

The Alabe Crafts Heyday

Throughout the 1950s, Alabe Crafts continued to produce innovative toys and novelties in addition to the Magic 8 Ball (which remained a company mainstay throughout). Around that time, a well-known local toy inventor, Don Poynter, began a long and fruitful association with Alabe.

Poynter had originally been acting as a one-man business, contracting with Japanese manufacturing plants to produce the

Dear Mattel . . .

There have been many Magic 8 Ball fan letters over the years, but one that stands out came from a woman who wrote in claiming she was known as "the Magic 8 Ball lady" in her town. She had a problem—suddenly her Magic 8 Ball had stopped providing the right answers! Her request was that Mattel send her a new one, only this time they "better make sure it was an accurate one!" Mattel sent her two replacements—but they made it clear there were no guarantees!

toys and novelties he came up with, but their track record with poor craftsmanship and lack of quality control were holding him back from being a success. When Abe Bookman and the Alabe team offered to work with him, overseeing his toys' construction and packaging at their usual high standards, Poynter knew a good thing when he saw it. And so began a long and fruitful Alabe Crafts/Don Poynter partnership, which led to some of the biggest sellers in the company's history.

Some of their popular items included:
◆ The Jayne Mansfield hot water bottle.
◆ Addams Family tie-ins like the Uncle Fester light bulb (hold it in your hand and it lights up!) and The Thing (a coin bank that "grabbed" your pennies).
◆ A cocktail holder and shaker in the shape of a girl; you placed your drink in her hand and she shook it for you.
◆ The Cigarette Donkey, with a push button mechanism that dispensed cigarettes out of his, er, derriere.

August is the traditional "rush time" in the toy business, as companies scramble to produce items for the Christmas season. Every summer, Alabe's shop would overflow with these and more colorful items rolling off the assembly line. Don Bookman remembers visiting his father's workplace and seeing all the rooms and hallways at the factory lined with stacked boxes upon boxes of Magic 8 Balls. Everyone in the company would pitch in on the assembly lines, especially important as several parts of the manufacturing were done by hand.

On the Assembly Line

Abe Bookman was always concerned with Alabe's reputation for quality. The high standards he set meant that the Magic 8 Ball casings were not simply two pieces of plastic glued together with an obvious seam. He felt that since the toys were marketed to adults as a conversation piece or desktop toy for executives, they should never look "cheap" but instead have a high level of workmanship evident in them.

Great care was taken to ensure the manufacturing process would produce a first-rate toy. First, the liquid filler, a combination of several ingredients including antifreeze, was heated to 140 degrees. At that temperature, the interior jars were filled and the floating polyhedron added to the liquid. The jars were capped while hot, and because they used a patented diaphragm that Abe designed, they expelled the excess air inside as the liquid cooled. Abe hated the idea of air bubbles in his Magic 8 Ball toys! Once the jar was cool, the two halves of the Magic 8 Ball casing were placed around it.

The two polystyrene shells were then cemented together clamped in a lathe, with the lathe operator using a flat blade to make the seam as smooth as possible. This step took some practice, but the lathe operators became experts. The final step was hand-buffing and polishing, so that the surface of the Magic 8 Ball was a perfect shiny sphere.

Magic 8 Balls for the Future?

THE MAGIC BAIT BALL

(For fishermen only!) Ever wonder what will work best on the end of your fishing pole? Wonder no more, the Magic Bait Ball is here to help! Ball features such answers as:

BASIC WORM
MEALWORM
NIGHTCRAWLER
HANDMADE LURE

Get ready for the catch of your life!

sta·ple

(stā′ pəl), *n., adj.*

A principal commodity in a mercantile field; goods
in steady demand or of known or recognized quality.

This standard dictionary definition is a pretty good description of Magic "8-Ball." For more than a
quarter-century, Magic "8-Ball" has been a **principal commodity** in the toy field creating a **steady
demand** and **recognized** as a **quality** item of exceptional play value. Today it is better than ever with
all-plastic safety construction plus bright new impulse-sales packaging. Its exciting sister item, ZODIAC
BALL for astrology and horoscope buffs, is making cash register music. Stock the items with all the
answers — Magic "8-Ball" and Zodiac Ball from Alabe.

Let the "8-Ball" get behind you!

alabe crafts inc. *1632 Gest Street • Cincinnati, Ohio 45204 • (513) 251-0886*

THE
Later Years

After the 1950s, the market for novelty toys like Don Poynter's
shrank. It also became harder and harder to maintain the level
of quality control that Alabe wanted, and there were many
frustrating years when the shoddy quality of some sub-
contracted goods reflected badly on the Alabe name.
In 1971, Alabe Crafts was sold to the Ideal Toy
company. Ideal continued to produce the Magic 8
Ball, and when they were acquired by Tyco Toys,
Inc. in 1987, Tyco carried on the proud tradition of

♦ Girls are going wild over the Magic Date Ball, a new spin on an old toy . . . The answers to such burning questions as "Does he like me?" never seemed so clear!

♦ Magic 8 Ball toys are now sold as miniature key chains. They work just like the original, but at a fraction of the size.

selling the ever-popular toy. In 1997, Tyco Toys joined the Mattel family.

In 1997, Tyco Toys introduced the Magic Date Ball™, a pink sphere with a new spin on the familiar fortune-telling mechanism. The Date Ball answers all your yes or no questions about love and dating, and was a big hit when it debuted at the industry toy fairs that year.

The official Mattel product line includes: The Magic 8 Ball, the Magic Date Ball, and The Magic Love Ball™.

It Is Decidedly So

It's been a long, interesting trip for the humble Magic 8 Ball. Many years have passed since 1946, when Max Levinson decided to

Let's Play . . .
The Magic 8 Ball Party Game!

Mattel introduced a Magic 8 Ball Party Game, a colorful game for 3 to 8 players (or teams). Fate and Fortune intersect to determine the winner, as players vie for tokens by answering questions or acting out scenes facilitated by the Fate and Fortune cards.

After going around the board with the help of the special Magic 8 Ball timer, a winner is declared. This winner is named the "Great 8 Potentate" and then the fun really begins! This Potentate calls the shots as the rest of the players try to win back tokens with their outrageous charades-style shenanigans.

Hooray For Hollywood

Unsurprisingly, the hit movie *Toy Story* was responsible for a surge in popularity and sales of classic toys like the Magic 8 Ball. By reminding the viewers of many of their favorite childhood toys, *Toy Story* created a run on such old favorites as Mr. Potato Head and Slinky. In *Toy Story*, Woody, the hero, consults his Magic 8 Ball for guidance before he sets off to save the day at Pizza Planet. Sure enough, after this movie was released, sales of Magic 8 Balls went up!

open his family business and sell novelty toys to the masses. Through the years, Abe Bookman and Sid Korey both helped Alabe Crafts produce a steadily-selling toy that engaged peoples' imaginations—not with lights or shiny gadgets but with simple old-fashioned fun. Let's ask the Magic 8 Ball itself about its staying power in the marketplace: Outlook good.

And why shouldn't the outlook be rosy? After all, this is a toy that continued to sell through many changes in design, from the unassuming jar of molasses Al Carter first invented to the

Lola comic strip.

shiny black sphere we know and love today. The Magic 8 Ball has survived through the post-war boom of the Fifties, the counterculture Sixties, The Me Decade Seventies, and so on–all the way to the new millennium and beyond.

Only one question remains. Will people continue their fascination with the supernatural? Will there always be room for a toy that amuses and enlightens with its simple yet perfect answers? To coin a phrase: It is decidedly so.

As Seen On TV!

Some memorable TV appearances of the Magic 8 Ball:

The Dick Van Dyke
  Show
Murphy Brown
Friends
The Simpsons
Dawson's Creek
Felicity
AT&T commercial
Dunkin' Donuts
  commercial

MAGIC 8 BALL
Fun Facts!

♦ President Eisenhower reputedly kept a Magic 8 Ball on his desk.
No word on whether he consulted it for matters of state.

♦ At Cincinnati restaurant Cristof's, tables are set with
Magic 8-Ball toys, to help diners decide what to order.

♦ In the hit movie *Toy Story*, the character of Woody consults
the Magic 8 Ball.

A Magic 8 Ball on every table at Cristof's.

- The original Magic 8-Ball prototype was a wooden cube in a jar filled with molasses.

- The Magic 8 Ball was featured in an AT&T commercial.

- In a survey of Americans on their favorite toys of the 20th century, the Magic 8 Ball ranked Number 20—between Chatty Cathy (19) and Creepy Crawlers (21).

- The number 8 has always had mystical properties. When turned on its side, it becomes the symbol for infinity

WILL
GRANDAD
VISIT?

WITHOUT A DOUBT.

TELL FORTUNES FOR YOUR FRIENDS!

MAGIC "8 BALL" ®
FORTUNE TELLER

ITEM NO. 2900-9
INSTRUCTIONS:

1. Ask a "Yes or No" question about future!

2. Turn ball over!

3. Read answer in window!

®

For ages 8 years and up. Fun for all.

alabe products, inc.
1632 Gest St.
Cincinnati, Ohio 45204

© PATENT NOS. 3119621, 3168315.   Made and printed in U.S.A.

THE MAGIC 8 BALL

Aptitude Test

1. The original prototype for the Magic 8 Ball was named:

     A. The Magic 6 Ball
     B. The Syco-Seer
     C. The Wonder Dog
     D. The Future-Globe

2. Alabe Crafts, the original Magic 8 Ball manufacturer, was located in:

    A. New York, NY
    B. Las Vegas, NV
    C. Minneapolis, MN
    D. Cincinnati, OH

3. The answer "cube" in the Magic 8 Ball has ____ sides.

    A. 20
    B. 12
    C. 9
    D. 6

4. The following President kept a Magic 8
   Ball on his desk:

   A. President Eisenhower
   B. President Nixon
   C. President Kennedy
   D. President Reagan

ASK A QUESTION

HAVE FUN TELLING FORTUNES!
. . . Magic, mysterious 8 ball answers all your questions! Just whisper question to the hidden genie; concentrate; and flip ball over. His answer appears in window at bottom. Tremendous fun with the future! "Starts the ball rolling" at parties. Shiny black plastic. 4" diam.
FORTUNE TELLING 8 BALL
(J-24810E) $1.98

TALKING TO
Past Celebrities

As I was working on this book, I had a brainstorm: Perhaps some historical figures would speak to me through the Magic 8 Ball! Below, some highlights from a series of interviews conducted by me, your author, over the course of the writing of this book. — MZ

MZ: Did you really chop down that cherry tree?

George Washington: Yes, definitely

MZ: Is it true that you died after a fan punched you in the stomach at your request?

Harry Houdini: Concentrate and ask again

MZ: All right, I'm asking again. Was that true?

Harry Houdini: Very doubtful

MZ: Will America have a woman president soon?

Susan B. Anthony: You may rely on it

MZ: Were you right about the future?

Nostradamus: Cannot predict now.

MZ: Is love really all you need?

John Lennon: Don't Count On It

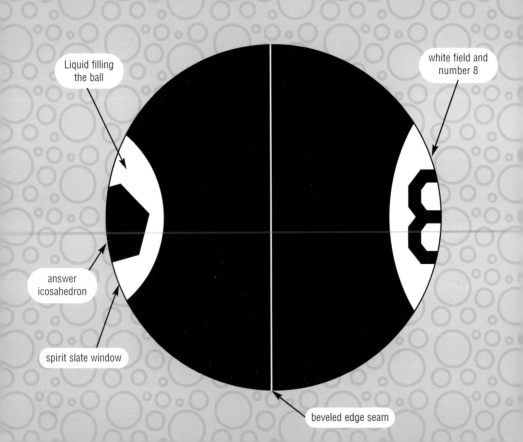

Liquid filling the ball

white field and number 8

answer icosahedron

spirit slate window

beveled edge seam

Terminology

Over the years, the design of the Magic 8 Ball has changed little.
One notable change was the beveled seam, which traditionally
had been sanded until smooth, giving the illusion of seamlessness.
The spirit slate window and the answer icosahedron, however,
have remained constant from the Magic 8 Ball's earliest days.